Date: 4/20/16

J 599.4 LEA
Leaf, Christina,
Brown bats /

NORTH AMERICAN ANIMALS

Brown Bats

by Christina Leaf

BELLWETHER MEDIA • MINNEAPOLIS, MN

Note to Librarians, Teachers, and Parents:

Blastoff! Readers are carefully developed by literacy experts and combine standards-based content with developmentally appropriate text.

Level 1 provides the most support through repetition of high-frequency words, light text, predictable sentence patterns, and strong visual support.

Level 2 offers early readers a bit more challenge through varied simple sentences, increased text load, and less repetition of high-frequency words.

Level 3 advances early-fluent readers toward fluency through increased text and concept load, less reliance on visuals, longer sentences, and more literary language.

Level 4 builds reading stamina by providing more text per page, increased use of punctuation, greater variation in sentence patterns, and increasingly challenging vocabulary.

Level 5 encourages children to move from "learning to read" to "reading to learn" by providing even more text, varied writing styles, and less familiar topics.

Whichever book is right for your reader, Blastoff! Readers are the perfect books to build confidence and encourage a love of reading that will last a lifetime!

This edition first published in 2016 by Bellwether Media, Inc.

No part of this publication may be reproduced in whole or in part without written permission of the publisher. For information regarding permission, write to Bellwether Media, Inc., Attention: Permissions Department, 5357 Penn Avenue South, Minneapolis, MN 55419.

Library of Congress Cataloging-in-Publication Data

Leaf, Christina, author.
  Brown Bats / by Christina Leaf.
     pages cm. – (Blastoff! Readers. North American Animals)
  Summary: "Simple text and full-color photography introduce beginning readers to brown bats. Developed by literacy experts for students in kindergarten through third grade"– Provided by publisher.
  Audience: Ages 5-8
  Audience: K to grade 3
  Includes bibliographical references and index.
  ISBN 978-1-62617-258-6 (hardcover: alk. paper)
  1. Bats–Juvenile literature. I. Title.
  QL737.C5L425 2016
  599.4–dc23
                                                      2014050318

Printed in the United States of America, North Mankato, MN.

Table of Contents

What Are Brown Bats?

Brown bats are flying **mammals**. They move through the air with **webbed wings**.

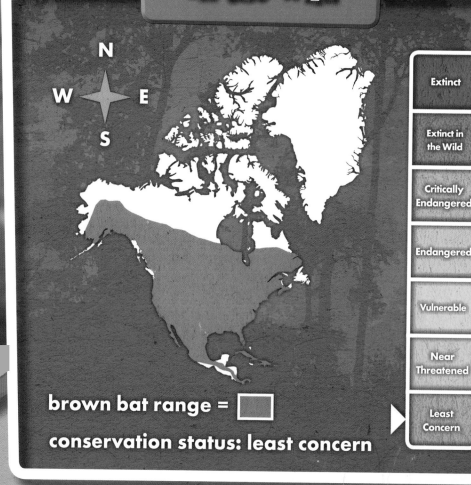

N
W E
S

brown bat range = ☐

conservation status: least concern

Extinct

Extinct in the Wild

Critically Endangered

Endangered

Vulnerable

Near Threatened

Least Concern

Brown bats are found all over North America except the far north. They often live near water in forests or swamps. Many also fly around cities or towns.

webbed wings   **brown fur**   **small ears**

Brown bats are named for the color of their fur. It can be dark, golden, or reddish brown.

The wings of a brown bat have no fur. They are usually black or dark brown.

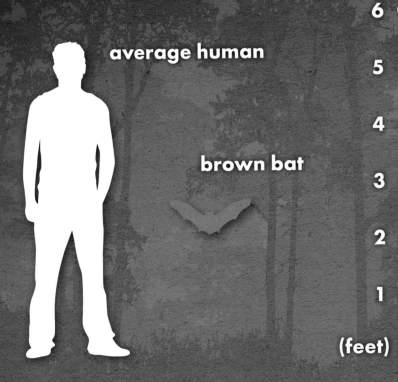

Size of a Brown Bat

average human

brown bat

6
5
4
3
2
1
(feet)

There are different sizes of brown bats. A little brown bat's wings measure up to 10 inches (25 centimeters) across.

The wings of a big brown bat are about 13 inches (33 centimeters) across.

At night, brown bats take flight. These hunters use **echolocation** to find **prey**.

They send sounds out into the dark. Then they listen. Echoes tell them how far away food is.

ground beetles

stinkbugs

mosquitoes

dragonflies

corn earworm moths

wasps

Brown bats are **insectivores**. They catch their dinner while they fly.

Many brown bats feast on beetles.
They also enjoy water insects.

After hunting, brown bats rest in **roosts**. They sleep hanging upside down. Their feet hold on tight.

house cats

fishers

great horned owls

raccoons

rat snakes

peregrine falcons

Brown bats hide to stay safe from **predators**. They roost in trees, on cliffs, or under bridges. Other favorite places are in barns or attics.

In fall, brown bats begin to **hibernate**. Most sleep through the winter in caves or mines. Some stay in houses or other buildings.

Little brown bats collect in big **colonies**. They cuddle together for heat. Big brown bats hibernate alone or in small groups.

Bat Pups

Brown bats leave hibernation in spring. Females gather together in **nursery** colonies. Mothers have one or two **pups** each year. They hang upright to give birth.

Baby Facts

Name for babies:	pups
Size of litter:	1 to 2 pups
Length of pregnancy:	7 months
Time spent with mom:	4 to 6 weeks

Pups can fly after about a month. They stay with mom for a few more weeks to practice hunting.

Then they take off into the night!

Glossary

colonies—groups of bats

echolocation—a process for locating objects by using sound waves reflected back to the sender by the object

hibernate—to spend the winter sleeping or resting

insectivores—animals that only eat insects

mammals—warm-blooded animals that have backbones and feed their young milk

nursery—a place where young bats are cared for

predators—animals that hunt other animals for food

prey—animals that are hunted by other animals for food

pups—baby brown bats

roosts—places where bats rest or sleep

webbed wings—wings made of bones connected by thin skin

To Learn More

AT THE LIBRARY

Carney, Elizabeth. *Bats*. Washington, D.C.: National Geographic, 2010.

Chrustowski, Rick. *Big Brown Bat*. New York, N.Y.: Henry Holt and Company, 2008.

Markovics, Joyce. *Little Brown Bats*. New York, N.Y.: Bearport Publishing, 2015.

ON THE WEB

Learning more about brown bats is as easy as 1, 2, 3.

1. Go to www.factsurfer.com.

2. Enter "brown bats" into the search box.

3. Click the "Surf" button and you will see a list of related web sites.

With factsurfer.com, finding more information is just a click away.

Index